SOCIAL JUSTICE AND YOU

BE A CHANGEMAKER

BY MARIBEL VALDEZ GONZALEZ

CAPSTONE PRESS
a capstone imprint

Published by Capstone Press, an imprint of Capstone
1710 Roe Crest Drive, North Mankato, Minnesota 56003
capstonepub.com

Library of Congress Cataloging-in-Publication Data
Names: Gonzalez, Maribel Valdez, author.
Title: Be a changemaker / by Maribel Valdez Gonzalez.
Description: North Mankato, Minnesota : Capstone Press, [2023] | Series: Social justice and you | Includes bibliographical references and index. | Audience: Ages 8–11 | Audience: Grades 4–6 | Summary: "What can you do when you know something is wrong? We're not always sure of the right thing to do. In this book, you'll learn about ways to speak up and step in when you recognize injustice in your community. With kid-friendly explanations of key ideas and relevant scenarios, this text will help young kids be changemakers in their community"— Provided by publisher.
Identifiers: LCCN 2022013070 (print) | LCCN 2022013071 (ebook) | ISBN 9781666345353 (hardcover) | ISBN 9781666345377 (paperback) | ISBN 9781666345384 (pdf) | ISBN 9781666345407 (kindle edition)
Subjects: LCSH: Social change—Juvenile literature. | Social action—Juvenile literature.
Classification: LCC HM831 .G683 2023 (print) | LCC HM831 (ebook) | DDC 303.4—dc23/eng/20220331
LC record available at https://lccn.loc.gov/2022013070
LC ebook record available at https://lccn.loc.gov/2022013071

Editorial Credits
Editor: Ericka Smith; Designer: Sarah Bennett; Media Researcher: Julie De Adder; Production Specialist: Katy LaVigne

Image Credits
Alamy: Bob Daemmrich Photography/Marjorie Kamys Cotera, 9, Patsy Lynch, 15, Reuters/Nicholas Pfosi, 12; Getty Images: Bettmann, 18, Jair Fonseca, 13, Jose Luis Pelaez Inc, 24; The New York Public Library: The Miriam and Ira D. Wallach Division of Art, Prints, and Photographs, 17; Shutterstock: 5D Media, 27, Allison C Bailey, 5, Atomazul, 8, bgrocker, 21, Eugene Powers, 20, Everett Collection, 10, Halfpoint, 29, Karin Hildebrand Lau, 11, Katerina Dalemans, 7, Magnia (background), back cover and throughout, Monkey Business Images, 19, Receh Lancar Jaya, cover, Rena Schild, 4, 6, 25, Sheila Fitzgerald, 22, 26, Vach cameraman, 23; ZUMA Press: San Antonio Express-News/San Antonio Light Collection at UTSA Special Collections, 16

All internet sites appearing in back matter were available and accurate when this book was sent to press.

TABLE OF CONTENTS

Words in **bold** are in the glossary.

WORKING TOWARD JUSTICE

Everyone should be able to thrive in their own community. That means we should be able to meet our basic needs. And we should also feel safe and respected.

But some of us experience unfair treatment and harm because of our identities. Identities are things like **class**, **race**, and age. Some people experience houselessness. **Indigenous** nations aren't always respected. And Black people are often victims of police violence. These kinds of injustices make it hard for people to feel supported, safe, and respected in their communities.

Young people work on art to support the Black Lives Matter movement.

For everyone to thrive in a community, people must work on change. A changemaker is someone who takes action to address injustice. They might organize protests, educate others, create artwork with a message, or even raise money to help address a problem.

CHAPTER 1

WHAT IS A CHANGEMAKER?

A changemaker addresses an injustice they experience or see. They work with people who are impacted by an injustice. They ask hard questions or challenge actions that cause harm. They use creativity to bring about change.

Changemakers are also **collaborative**. They build relationships with others. They respect others and their experiences. And they work with others to come up with ways to take action.

IDEAS IN ACTION

Jonathan's brother Mark came out as gay to his family. Mark told Jonathan that he was afraid his classmates might find out he is gay. He was worried about being bullied.

Jonathan goes to the same school as Mark. Jonathan decided to use art to bring awareness to different sexual identities at school. During art class, he and his friends created posters that read "Be who you are!" and showed the pride flag. They put the posters up in the hallway. This got kids and teachers talking about being more accepting of **queer** people at school and in their community.

What action did Jonathan take?

How did this action change Jonathan and Mark's school?

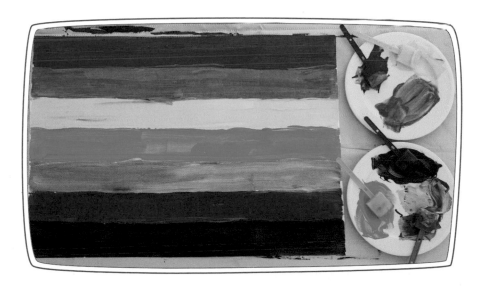

Changemakers take on all kinds of problems. Sometimes they take big steps toward change. They might talk to a school principal about changing a dress code that excludes students of color. They might organize a **strike** to get better pay for workers. Or they might build homes for people who need housing.

Changemakers can also take smaller steps toward change. They might organize a food drive for a local food bank. Or they might start a support group for queer students. Small steps can help people feel cared for.

IDEAS IN ACTION

Rita learned in their social studies class that thousands of people in their city sometimes stay in shelters when they don't have a place to live. With help from their teacher and classmates, Rita came up with an idea to support people experiencing houselessness. They could organize a food drive for a local shelter.

Rita's social studies teacher, Mrs. Garcia, suggested that Rita talk to the principal about their idea. Rita met with the principal, Mrs. Thomas, and she liked Rita's idea. She helped Rita and their classmates organize the food drive.

What is the problem Rita wants to address?

What steps did Rita take to make a change in their community?

CHAPTER 2

WHO ARE SOME CHANGEMAKERS?

Changemakers—past and present—stand up for what they believe in. They do different things to address the injustice they or others experience. And sometimes they experience harm for fighting back.

Women advocating for the right to vote in 1918

Learning about changemakers can inspire us. Knowing what others have done or are doing to fight injustice helps us see ways to take action ourselves. It also helps us understand that some of the rights we have today are the result of changemakers' actions. Being a changemaker is not always easy. But it is important.

WINONA LADUKE

Winona LaDuke is an **Anishinaabe activist**. She fights for Indigenous people to have control over their land, medicine, and traditions. LaDuke is also a founder and leader of Honor the Earth. This organization helped delay the construction of the Line 3 pipeline in Minnesota.

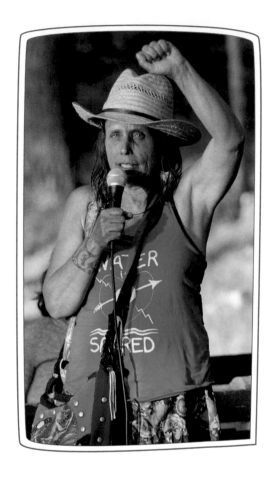

The Line 3 pipeline carries oil from Canada through Minnesota to Wisconsin. It could destroy the wild rice beds of the Anishinaabe peoples. LaDuke and her community tried to prevent this from happening. They did this by organizing a march to the state capitol, asking state officials to stop construction, submitting **petitions**, and holding events to bring awareness to the issue.

FIGHTING DEFORESTATION IN THE AMAZON

Yurshell Rodríguez is a member of the **Raizal** ethnic group of the Colombian island Providencia. Rodríguez is trying to protect her home and prevent the effects of climate change. She was part of a group of youth activists who sued the Colombian government for failing to stop deforestation—the removal of trees for things like farming and lumber—in the Amazon. The trees of the Amazon are important because they help cool the air and reduce carbon dioxide in the air. The group won the lawsuit in 2018, but deforestation has increased. Still, Rodríguez is continuing her activism.

MARSHA P. JOHNSON

Marsha P. Johnson was a Black drag queen, activist, and performer in New York City. She participated in the Stonewall Uprising of 1969. She also helped found a group called STAR. She started it with her friend Sylvia Rivera. They helped provide shelter and services for LGBTQIA+ youth.

In 1970, New York University (NYU) canceled a dance because it was sponsored by a gay organization. The LGBTQIA+ community protested their decision. Students and activists, including Johnson, organized a sit-in. A sit-in is a form of protest during which people refuse to move from where they are until their demands are met. The protesters sent a powerful message to NYU that the university should care about the needs of the LGBTQIA+ community. And Johnson and Rivera got the idea for STAR during this sit-in.

 FACT LGBTQIA+ stands for lesbian, gay, bisexual, transgender, queer, intersex, and asexual. The plus sign means that there are other gender and sexual identities that may not be covered by the other terms.

EMMA TENAYUCA

Emma Tenayuca was a Mexican American activist and labor organizer in San Antonio, Texas. In 1938, pecan companies planned to lower workers' pay. Tenayuca helped the workers organize a strike. A strike is when employees stop working until their demands are met.

The strike included about 12,000 workers. It lasted for three months. The police tried to stop the strikers. They used tear gas and clubs, but the strikers did not give in.

FACT Most of the shellers at pecan companies were Mexican and Mexican American women. Before the company threatened to lower wages, they were working more than 10 hours a day, seven days a week, in poor conditions. They earned only $2 to $3 a week.

Workers in a pecan factory in San Antonio

The strike ended with a compromise. The workers did earn higher pay. But over time, many workers were replaced by machines.

The strike changed how people viewed workers' power. In fact, the next mayor of San Antonio was someone who had supported the strike.

ED ROBERTS

In 1962, Ed Roberts was the first student who used a wheelchair to attend the University of California (UC), Berkeley. When he was 14 years old, Roberts contracted polio. It left him paralyzed from the neck down. He needed a machine to help him breathe.

After Roberts was accepted to the university, administrators learned about his disability. They tried to change their decision. They said that the machine he needed to breathe wouldn't fit into the dorms.

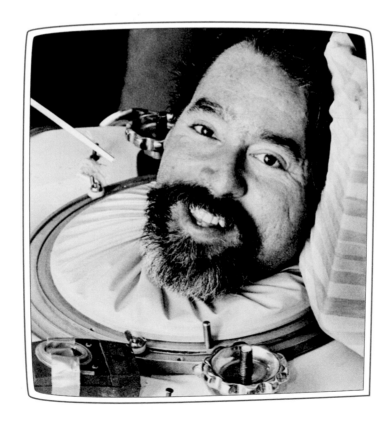

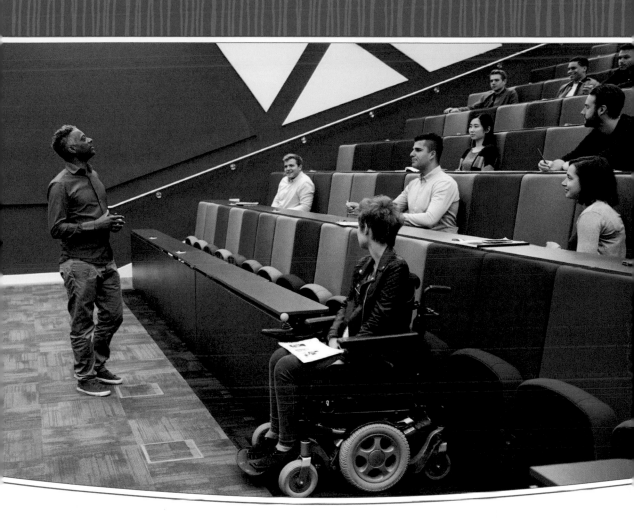

That didn't stop Roberts. He kept fighting and was offered housing in part of the university's hospital, where he could use the machine he needed to breathe.

Over time, more people with disabilities attended the university. With Ed Roberts's leadership, UC Berkeley learned to provide **accommodations** to students with disabilities. Other universities followed and began to accept students with disabilities.

AMANDA NGUYEN

Amanda Nguyen is a Vietnamese American activist who founded the nonprofit organization Rise. In 2021, Nguyen noticed that the hate and violence the Asian community was experiencing was not being reported in the news. So she took action.

On February 5, 2021, Nguyen posted a video on Instagram. She asked national news outlets to cover the anti-Asian hate against older Asian people in places like San Francisco and New York City. The video went viral. It had millions of views and was shared on social media platforms. As a result, networks like ABC and CNN asked Nguyen to speak about the problem.

Nguyen's effort to draw attention to the problem was successful. Her decision to post a video became an important moment for the Stop Asian Hate movement.

CHAPTER 3

HOW CAN I BE A CHANGEMAKER?

What changes do you want to make in your community? What injustices have you seen or experienced that make you sad or angry? What would help you feel safe, supported, and respected?

If you're affected by an issue you choose to address, you'll have a clearer understanding of the problem. If the issue doesn't affect you, you should be careful when deciding what action to take. Make sure you are following the lead of people who are affected.

IDEAS IN ACTION

Adrian is a Jewish fifth grader. He wanted to show his support for the Black Lives Matter movement. He saw other students with different racial and ethnic identities wearing Black Lives Matter T-shirts. He decided to wear his Black Lives Matter T-shirt to school too.

When his Latino friend Anthony saw him in it, he made a face. "Don't all lives matter?"

Adrian replied, "All lives matter when Black lives matter. This is a call for justice from the Black community. It doesn't mean only Black lives matter. It means they should matter in the United States too."

Anthony took a minute to think about what Adrian said. Then, he replied, "True."

How does Adrian show support for the Black Lives Matter movement?

Why is Adrian's conversation with his friend Anthony important?

First, learn as much as you can about the problem. What is the problem? What causes the problem? Who is affected? Are other people trying to solve it? What are they doing? Should you join them? Should you try a different approach?

Then, start making decisions about what to do. There are many ways you can create change. It depends on what you want to happen. Some changes can happen quickly. Others take a lot of time. Here are a few ideas:

- **Raise awareness.** This means that you want more people to know about the issue. Amanda Nguyen helped bring awareness to anti-Asian hate.

- **Provide a service.** This means that you help people get something they need. Marsha P. Johnson's STAR organization helped provide housing for queer youth.

- **Get a practice, rule, or law changed.** This means that you want some group—a community, an organization, or the government—to change. Ed Roberts helped change UC Berkeley's services for students with disabilities.

Remember, your actions can be big or small. All steps toward justice are valuable.

Once you've decided which approach to take, think about specific actions you can take and discuss them with a trusted adult. How will you draw attention to an issue? What do you want to do for people? How will you change the minds of lawmakers? Changemakers use different ways to make an impact:

- creating art with a message
- submitting petitions
- organizing marches
- talking to the media
- raising money for an organization
- talking to people in government
- asking people to vote for a new law

Movements are stronger when more people's voices are included. Think about who you can work with to create change and impact as many people as possible. How can you inspire those people to join your cause?

MAKE A PLAN

To create a plan for action, try answering these questions:

- What do I want to happen?
- What do I need to do to make that change?
- Who else should I include?

We should all live in communities where everyone feels safe, supported, and respected. But many people experience injustice.

Everyone can help make our world a better place. So when you experience or see injustice, make the choice to take action. You can take big steps or little steps toward change. Any step forward is valuable.

Being a changemaker can have a huge effect on you, your community, and the world. What injustice will you help change?

FACT Many young people are using social media to educate themselves and others about issues ranging from racial justice to climate change. Social media is a powerful way to demand change and create awareness about issues you care about.

GLOSSARY

accommodation (uh-kom-uh-DAY-shuhn)—a change made to meet the needs of someone with a disability

activist (AK-tuh-vist)—a person who works for social or political change

Anishinaabe (uh-nish-uh-nah-BAY)—belonging to an Indigenous group that lives in parts of Canada, Minnesota, Wisconsin, Michigan, and North Dakota

class (KLASS)—a group of people in society with a similar way of life or range of income

collaborative (kuh-LAB-er-uh-tiv)—likely to work with others instead of alone

Indigenous (in-DIJ-uh-nuss)—belonging to the group of people who first lived in a place

Latine (la-TEE-neh)—from or having ancestors from a country in Latin America, such as the Dominican Republic, Mexico, or Chile

petition (puh-TISH-uhn)—a letter signed by many people asking leaders for a change

queer (KWEER)—holding identities such as lesbian, gay, bisexual, pansexual, and transgender; identifying as something other than heterosexual or cisgender

race (RAYSS)—groups into which humans have been divided based on shared physical traits; these broad categories have been created to benefit some groups

Raizal (RAI-sahl)—an Afro-Caribbean ethnic group that lives on a group of Colombian islands

strike (STRIKE)—refusing to work because of a disagreement with an employer over wages or working conditions

READ MORE

Hudson, Wade, and Cheryl Willis Hudson, eds. *We Rise, We Resist, We Raise Our Voices.* New York: Yearling, 2018.

Saunders, Claire, Hazel Songhurst, Georgia Amson-Bradshaw, Minna Salami, and Mik Scarlet. *The Power Book: What Is It, Who Has It, and Why?* London: Ivy Kids, 2019.

Stevenson, Robin. *Kid Activists: True Tales of Childhood from Champions of Change.* Philadelphia: Quirk Books, 2019.

INTERNET SITES

Ashoka Youth Years: Young Changemakers
ashokayouthyears.org/young-changemakers/

Our Kids Series: Why I Organize
ourkidsseries.org/blog-detail/10/why-i-organize/

PBS: Kids Can Be Changemakers
www.pbslearningmedia.org/resource/kids-can-be-changemakers-video/meet-the-helpers/

INDEX

ABOUT THE AUTHOR

Maribel Valdez Gonzalez is an Indigenous Xicana STEM/PBL coach, former classroom teacher, and consultant. She resides in occupied Duwamish territory, also known as Seattle, Washington. She is from occupied Somi Se'k land, also known as San Antonio, Texas. In her 10 years as an antiracist educator, Maribel has been honored to work with youth and adults to decolonize and humanize teaching practices and belief systems in classrooms and beyond. Maribel's goal is to create academically engaging learning experiences through a culturally sustaining environment that fosters empowerment, healing, and radical kindness. She is also a member of the Antiracist Arts Education Task Force for Visual & Performing Arts in Seattle Public Schools.